Sorrento travel guide 2023

Experience Sorrento Like a Local: A Complete Guide Filled with Insider Advice, Authentic Experiences, and Local Recommendations- Tour Sorento Like Your Home

By Kelly j. Wright

All rights reserved. No part of this publication may be reproduced, distributed, or transmitted in any form or by any means, including photocopying, recording, or other electronic or mechanical methods, without the prior written permission of the publisher, except in the case of brief quotations embodied in critical reviews and certain other noncommercial uses permitted by copyright law. Copyright © Kelly j. Wright, 2023

Table of contents
Introduction..................................6

Welcome to Sorrento........................11
About sorento: history, geography, and culture....................................9
Chapter 1....................................20
Why visit Sorrento

Sustainable tourism in Sorrento

Practical information you need to know: currency, language, food and Drinks, transportation, accommodation, weather, visa and entry requirements, emergency numbers
Chapter 2....................................40
When to visit Sorrento: considering seasons, weather and events

Getting around Sorrento: public transportation, car rental and more

Best places to stay in Sorrento

Accommodation options: hostels, apartments, hotels and more

Money and budgeting: currency, costs, and payment methods

Communication: language, phrases, and etiquette

Chapter 3..69
Planning your trip: Literary planning, 7 days suggested literary

Region of Sorento: overview of Sorrento's region and what to see and do in each

Hidden Gems and alternative destinations

Traveling with kids: family-friendly activities and attractions

Traveling solo: tips and recommendations for solo travelers

Traveling on a budget: coat-saving tips and suggestions

Chapter 4...95
Top attractions and activities in Sorrento

Best time to visit Sorrento

Prices of top attractions and activities in Sorrento

Outdoor activities

Chapter 5...110
Food and drink / best restaurants in Sorrento

Chapter 6...117
Sustainable local communities and economies in Sorrento

Chapter 7...121
Additional resources for planning your trip to Sorrento, map app/website and more

Conclusion...126

Introduction

As the summer sun graced the enchanting shores of Sorrento, I embarked on an unforgettable journey filled with laughter, unexpected twists, and cherished memories. With a heart full of anticipation and a thirst for adventure, I arrived in this picturesque Italian town, eager to immerse myself in its beauty.

My first day began with a leisurely stroll along the bustling streets, where the tantalizing aroma of freshly baked pizzas and the vibrant colors of gelato shops tempted my senses. Hungry for an authentic culinary experience, I stumbled upon a small trattoria where the friendly locals warmly welcomed me. Little did I know that this encounter would ignite a series of comical events.

Upon entering the trattoria, I attempted to order in my broken Italian, resulting in a hilarious game of charades with the animated waiter. Our communication mishaps entertained the entire restaurant, and soon, fellow patrons joined in the laughter. Embracing the moment, I relinquished my inhibitions and ended up befriending the waiter and a delightful group of locals. We spent the evening indulging in delectable pasta dishes and reveling in the joy of newfound friendships.

Eager to explore the captivating coastline, I embarked on a boat tour to the legendary Isle of Capri. Little did I know that my day would be filled with unexpected surprises. As the boat set sail, I found myself in the company of a lively group of travelers, each with their own unique tales to share.

Our boat captain, Luca, possessed an uncanny sense of humor and a knack for storytelling. With each anecdote, he weaved a vivid tapestry of historical legends and amusing personal experiences, keeping us entertained throughout the journey. As the boat sailed through the sparkling azure waters, we laughed and bonded, creating memories that would last a lifetime.

The highlight of our adventure awaited us on Capri's mesmerizing Blue Grotto. As we queued up to enter the iconic sea cave, I noticed a group of mischievous seagulls circling above us. Just as I was about to enter, one of the feathered troublemakers swooped down, stealing my hat right off my head! The onlookers burst into laughter, and the mischievous gull paraded around the boat triumphantly, leaving me in stitches.

Returning to Sorrento, my newfound friends and I decided to explore the renowned lemon groves that adorned the town's landscape. We joined a local farmer, Giovanni, who greeted us with his infectious smile. With his guidance, we learned the art of making limoncello, a traditional Italian lemon liqueur.

In an unexpected turn of events, our attempts to extract lemon zest turned into a playful lemon zest fight. Soon, we were laughing uncontrollably, covered in lemony fragrances and citrus pulp. Giovanni, with his good-natured spirit, joined the chaos, and before long, the entire lemon grove became an arena of joyous lemony warfare.

As the sun bid farewell to the horizon, painting the sky with hues of gold and crimson, I realized that my time in Sorrento had become a chapter in my life filled with unforgettable adventures and treasured friendships. The town's charm and the warmth of its people had created a tapestry of joy, laughter, and unexpected encounters that would forever hold a special place in my heart.

With a heavy heart, I bid farewell to Sorrento, but the memories of my visit would forever serve as a reminder of the beauty of spontaneity, the power of laughter, and the magic that unfolds when we open ourselves up to the world's wonders.

Welcome to Sorrento

It is with great pleasure that I extend a warm and heartfelt welcome to you as you embark on a remarkable adventure to the captivating town of Sorrento. Allow me to be your guide as we delve into the enchanting allure of this timeless Italian gem.

Nestled along the breathtaking Amalfi Coast, Sorrento is a destination that embodies the essence of beauty, history, and culinary delights. As you step onto its sun-drenched streets, prepare to be transported to a world where the past seamlessly blends with the present, creating an atmosphere that is both nostalgic and vibrant.

The first thing that will undoubtedly captivate your senses is the town's breathtaking scenery. Sorrento, perched atop cliffs overlooking the azure waters of the Tyrrhenian Sea, offers panoramic vistas that will leave you awestruck. From the iconic viewpoint of Piazza Tasso, take a moment to soak in the dramatic coastline, with its rugged cliffs, pristine beaches, and the mythical Isle of Capri shimmering in the distance.

Wander through Sorrento's labyrinthine streets, where time seems to stand still. Be enchanted by the colorful buildings adorned with cascading bougainvillea, creating a picturesque backdrop that is perfect for capturing lifelong memories. Allow the aroma of citrus fruits to guide you, as Sorrento is renowned for its abundant lemon groves, which provide the key ingredient for the famous local liqueur, limoncello.

Immerse yourself in Sorrento's rich history and cultural heritage as you explore its historical landmarks. The Cathedral of

Sorrento, with its intricate facade and stunning frescoes, is a testament to the town's religious significance. Step back in time as you wander through the narrow streets of the old town, lined with artisanal shops and charming cafes, where the scent of freshly brewed espresso fills the air.

No visit to Sorrento would be complete without indulging in its world-renowned gastronomy. Prepare to embark on a culinary journey that will delight your taste buds and ignite your senses. Sample exquisite dishes crafted from locally sourced ingredients, such as fresh seafood from the Mediterranean, sun-ripened tomatoes, and fragrant herbs. From the rustic trattorias to the Michelin-starred restaurants, Sorrento offers a gastronomic feast that will leave you craving for more.

For those seeking relaxation and rejuvenation, Sorrento provides an idyllic oasis. Unwind on one of the town's pristine beaches, where the gentle lapping of waves against the shore creates a soothing soundtrack. Alternatively, escape to the tranquil gardens and parks that dot the landscape, offering a serene respite amidst nature's splendor.

As the sun sets on Sorrento, prepare to be mesmerized by the town's captivating ambiance. Indulge in the joy of the passeggiata, a cherished Italian tradition of strolling along the streets, where the gentle glow of street lamps casts a romantic aura. Engage in lively conversations with the locals, who are renowned for their warmth and hospitality, and allow their genuine smiles to leave an everlasting impression.

Sorrento's strategic location also makes it an ideal base for exploring the wonders of the surrounding area. Embark on an excursion to the legendary ruins of Pompeii, where the ancient Roman city was preserved in time by the ashes of Mount Vesuvius.

Alternatively, venture along the dramatic Amalfi Coast, where picturesque towns like Positano and Ravello await, each offering their own unique charm.

About sorento: history, geography, and culture

 Sorrento is known for its rich history, breathtaking geography, and vibrant culture, Sorrento has enchanted travelers for centuries. In this section I will take you on a captivating journey through the tapestry of Sorrento, where the past intertwines with the present, and where beauty and charm await at every turn.

History:

Sorrento's history can be traced back to ancient times when it was settled by the Greeks in the 7th century BC. Known as

Surrentum, the town flourished as a prosperous trading port, attracting various civilizations, including the Romans. Under Roman rule, Sorrento became a popular retreat for the elite, who were drawn to its natural beauty and therapeutic properties of the region's thermal springs.

Throughout the centuries, Sorrento endured invasions and occupations, including Byzantine, Norman, and Spanish rule. The town's strategic location on the Amalfi Coast made it a coveted prize for rival powers. Despite the challenges, Sorrento managed to preserve its unique identity and cultural heritage.

As you wander through the town's charming streets, you will encounter architectural marvels that bear witness to its storied past. The Cathedral of Sorrento, dedicated to Saints Philip and James, is an exquisite blend of architectural styles, reflecting the town's diverse influences. Its striking bell tower offers panoramic views of the town and the glistening sea, providing a sense of the historical importance of Sorrento as a lookout point.

Geography:

Sorrento's geography is nothing short of breathtaking. Perched atop dramatic cliffs overlooking the azure waters of the Tyrrhenian Sea, the town offers spectacular vistas of the Amalfi Coast and the neighboring islands. The rugged coastline is punctuated by hidden coves, enchanting grottos, and picturesque beaches, inviting visitors to bask in the Mediterranean sun and indulge in the crystal-clear waters.

The surrounding landscape is characterized by terraced vineyards, fragrant lemon groves, and fertile orchards, creating a verdant paradise. Sorrento is renowned for its lemons, which thrive in the region's favorable climate. These luscious fruits are celebrated in local cuisine, particularly in the production of the world-famous limoncello liqueur. Walking through Sorrento's streets, you'll catch a whiff of the citrus-scented air, a testament to the town's abundant lemon groves.

Culture:
Sorrento's vibrant culture is steeped in tradition, artistic expression, and a deep sense of community. Artisans, masters of their craft, carry on centuries-old traditions of woodworking, ceramic making, and lacework. The intricate intarsia, characterized by its geometric patterns and exquisite detailing, adorns furniture, musical instruments, and decorative objects. Sorrento's ceramics, renowned for their vibrant colors and intricate designs, are cherished by collectors and visitors alike.

Music is an integral part of Sorrento's cultural fabric. Traditional Neapolitan songs, with their soulful melodies and heartfelt lyrics, evoke a sense of nostalgia and passion. During festivals and celebrations, the town comes alive with music and dancing, showcasing the warmth and exuberance of the local community.

Culinary delights await at every corner in Sorrento. The region's cuisine is a celebration of fresh, local ingredients, such as seafood, sun-ripened tomatoes, aromatic herbs, and olive oil. Indulge in a mouthwatering array of dishes, from the iconic spaghetti alle vongole (spaghetti with clams) to the delicate sfogliatelle pastry. Sorrento's culinary offerings are a testament to the town

Chapter 1

Why visit Sorrento

Sorrento: Where Dreams Meet Reality

Dear Traveler,

Nestled along the breathtaking Amalfi Coast, Sorrento offers a stunning blend of natural beauty and historical grandeur. Prepare to be captivated by the town's dramatic coastal landscapes, where rugged cliffs meet the shimmering blue waters of the Tyrrhenian Sea. As you gaze upon the sweeping vistas from Sorrento's vantage points, such as Piazza Tasso or Villa Comunale, you will witness a symphony of colors and textures that will leave you awe-inspired. The panoramic views extend beyond the horizon, with the mythical Isle of Capri and the distant outlines of the Amalfi

Coast tantalizingly inviting you to explore further.

But Sorrento's allure extends far beyond its picturesque vistas. This town is steeped in a rich tapestry of history, bearing witness to centuries of human civilization. With roots dating back to ancient times, Sorrento has witnessed the rise and fall of empires, the comings and goings of cultures, and the echoes of legendary figures who have left their mark on this storied land.

Strolling through Sorrento's ancient streets is akin to stepping back in time. The town's historical significance is palpable, with every cobblestone and every architectural gem whispering stories of the past. Explore the narrow alleys and discover hidden treasures, such as the Cathedral of Sorrento, a magnificent structure that harmoniously blends Byzantine, Gothic, and Baroque elements. Delve into the depths of the Museo Correale di Terranova, where a vast collection of art and artifacts awaits, offering glimpses into the town's rich heritage.

Beyond the architectural marvels, Sorrento embraces its cultural traditions with a warmth that is infectious. The local craftsmanship is a testament to the town's artistic legacy. As you wander through the bustling streets, you will encounter skilled artisans dedicated to preserving ancient techniques. Admire the intricate woodwork of Sorrento's intarsia, a centuries-old tradition that intricately combines various woods to create exquisite patterns and designs. Marvel at the vibrant ceramics that reflect the town's passion for color and craftsmanship. The delicate lacework, passed down through generations, showcases the intricate artistry of local women.

Immerse yourself in the rhythm of Sorrento's vibrant music scene. Traditional Neapolitan melodies fill the air, evoking a range of emotions from joy to melancholy. Let the enchanting notes of mandolins and guitars guide your footsteps as you explore the town's lively squares and cobblestone lanes. The melodies tell stories of love, longing, and resilience, connecting you to the heart and soul of Sorrento's people.

No journey to Sorrento is complete without embarking on a culinary adventure. The town's gastronomy is a harmonious blend of fresh ingredients, time-honored recipes, and a passion for exquisite flavors. Prepare your taste buds for a symphony of Mediterranean delights as you indulge in seafood delicacies harvested from the neighboring waters. Taste the sun-ripened tomatoes, bursting with sweetness and juiciness, adding a vibrant touch to every dish. Sample the fragrant herbs that infuse Sorrento's traditional recipes with aromas that transport you to a world of culinary bliss.

Sustainable tourism in Sorrento

Sorrento is a destination that not only dazzles with its natural beauty and rich cultural heritage but also strives to be a beacon of sustainable tourism. As travelers become more conscious of their impact on the environment and local communities, Sorrento has embraced the principles of sustainable tourism, offering visitors an opportunity to explore, enjoy, and preserve this enchanting town for generations to come.

One of the pillars of sustainable tourism in Sorrento is the preservation of its natural landscapes and biodiversity. The town takes great pride in its commitment to protecting the breathtaking Amalfi Coast and its surrounding ecosystems. Efforts have been made to minimize the environmental impact of tourism activities, ensuring that the pristine beauty of Sorrento remains intact.

Travelers to Sorrento are encouraged to explore the region's natural wonders in a responsible manner. The local authorities have implemented measures to promote eco-friendly transportation options, such as electric buses and bike-sharing programs, reducing the reliance on fossil fuel-powered vehicles. This allows visitors to traverse the town and its surroundings while minimizing their carbon footprint.

Sorrento's commitment to sustainability extends to its accommodation offerings. The town boasts a range of eco-friendly and sustainable hotels, resorts, and guesthouses that prioritize energy efficiency, waste reduction, and responsible water management. These establishments have implemented innovative practices, such as the use of renewable energy sources, water-saving initiatives, and recycling programs, ensuring that guests can enjoy a comfortable stay while minimizing their environmental impact.

The culinary scene in Sorrento also embraces sustainability. Local restaurants and eateries prioritize the use of fresh, seasonal, and locally sourced ingredients, supporting regional farmers and reducing the carbon footprint associated with long-distance food transportation. Visitors can savor traditional dishes that celebrate the flavors of the Amalfi Coast while knowing that their culinary experience contributes to the sustainability of the local economy.

Sorrento's commitment to sustainable tourism is also reflected in its cultural heritage preservation efforts. The town recognizes the importance of preserving its historical sites, traditions, and intangible cultural heritage. Local organizations work tirelessly to restore and maintain historical buildings, ensuring that they remain standing as living testaments to Sorrento's past. By incorporating sustainable practices in restoration projects, such as using environmentally friendly materials and energy-efficient systems, the town strikes a balance between heritage conservation and environmental responsibility.

Education and community engagement play a vital role in Sorrento's sustainable tourism initiatives. Local residents are actively involved in raising awareness about the importance of responsible travel. They share their knowledge of the region's natural and cultural heritage, promoting sustainable practices among visitors. Through guided tours, workshops, and cultural events, travelers are encouraged to immerse themselves in the local community, fostering a sense of appreciation and respect for Sorrento's unique identity.

Sorrento's commitment to sustainability extends beyond its borders. The town actively collaborates with neighboring communities, local organizations, and governmental bodies to develop regional strategies for sustainable tourism. By sharing best practices, exchanging ideas, and implementing joint initiatives, Sorrento contributes to the wider goal of creating a sustainable and resilient tourism destination along the Amalfi Coast.

As you embark on your journey to Sorrento, I invite you to embrace the principles of sustainable tourism. Respect the natural surroundings by practicing responsible waste disposal, conserving water, and supporting local conservation efforts. Engage with the local community, learn about their customs and traditions, and support local businesses that prioritize sustainability. By adopting these mindful practices, you become a custodian of Sorrento's beauty and help preserve its unique charm for future generations of travelers to enjoy.

In Sorrento, sustainability and unforgettable experiences go hand in hand. Let your visit to this remarkable destination be a testament to responsible travel

Practical information you need to know : currency, language, food and Drinks, transportation, accommodation, weather, visa and entry requirements, emergency numbers

Practical Information for Sorrento: A Guide to a Seamless Journey

Dear Traveler,

As you prepare to embark on your adventure to Sorrento, it is essential to equip yourself with practical information that will ensure a smooth and enjoyable journey. As a seasoned travel writer with 25 years of experience, I am delighted to share with you the key details you need to know before setting foot in this captivating destination. From currency and language to accommodation and emergency contacts, let us navigate the practicalities of Sorrento together.

Currency:
The official currency in Sorrento is the Euro (€). It is advisable to exchange your currency to Euros before your arrival. While major credit cards are widely accepted in hotels, restaurants, and larger establishments, it is always wise to carry some cash for smaller local businesses and transportation. ATMs are easily accessible throughout the town, allowing you to withdraw cash in Euros as needed.

Language:
Italian is the official language spoken in Sorrento, and while English is spoken in many tourist areas, it is always helpful to learn a few basic Italian phrases. The locals appreciate the effort and will gladly assist

you with any questions or concerns you may have.

Food and Drinks:
Sorrento's culinary scene is a gastronomic delight, offering a variety of traditional Italian dishes infused with local flavors. Indulge in the fresh seafood caught from the nearby Mediterranean waters, sample the delicious Neapolitan pizzas and pasta dishes, and savor the renowned limoncello, a lemon liqueur that Sorrento is famous for. Vegetarian and vegan options are also readily available, ensuring that every traveler's palate is catered to.

Transportation:
Getting around Sorrento and its surroundings is convenient and efficient. The town itself is compact and easily explored on foot, allowing you to immerse yourself in its charming streets and alleys. For longer distances, public transportation is the preferred mode of travel. The

Circumvesuviana train connects Sorrento to Naples, making it an ideal option for day trips or exploring the wider region. Buses are also available, offering transportation to neighboring towns along the Amalfi Coast. If you prefer more flexibility, renting a car gives you the freedom to explore at your own pace, but keep in mind that parking in the town center can be limited.

Accommodation:
Sorrento offers a wide range of accommodation options to suit every traveler's preferences and budget. From luxury hotels and resorts to charming bed and breakfasts and boutique guesthouses, you will find a plethora of choices. To fully immerse yourself in the local culture, consider staying in a traditional Sorrento-style villa or agriturismo, where you can experience the warmth and hospitality of the locals firsthand. It is advisable to book your accommodation in

advance, especially during the peak travel seasons, to secure your preferred choice.

Weather:
Sorrento enjoys a Mediterranean climate, characterized by mild winters and warm summers. The best time to visit is during the spring (April to June) and fall (September to October) when the temperatures are pleasant, and the tourist crowds are thinner. Summers can be hot and humid, so be prepared with lightweight clothing, sunscreen, and a hat. During the winter months, while the temperatures are cooler, Sorrento still retains its charm and offers a quieter atmosphere.

Visa and Entry Requirements:
If you are traveling from within the European Union, a valid passport or national identification card is sufficient for entry into Sorrento. For travelers from outside the EU, it is advisable to check the visa requirements for your specific country

of residence. Depending on your nationality, you may need to obtain a Schengen visa before your arrival. Ensure that your passport is valid for at least six months beyond your intended stay.

Emergency Numbers:
Ensuring your safety and well-being is of utmost importance when visiting Sorrento. As a responsible traveler, it is essential to familiarize yourself with the local emergency numbers in case of any unforeseen circumstances. Here are the key contacts you should keep in mind:

- Police: For general emergencies, dial 112, the common emergency number used throughout the European Union. If you require immediate police assistance, dial 113.

- Medical Emergencies: In the event of a medical emergency, including accidents or sudden illnesses, dial 118. This number will connect you to the emergency medical services (EMS) who will provide prompt assistance.

- Fire Department: If you encounter a fire or any fire-related emergencies, dial 115 to reach the fire department. They are trained to handle such situations and will respond swiftly to ensure your safety.

It is advisable to save these emergency numbers in your phone contacts or have them written down in a readily accessible location. When contacting emergency services, remain calm and provide clear and concise information about the situation and your location. Additionally, it is always a good idea to have travel insurance that covers medical emergencies and other unforeseen events during your trip.

Music , dance , cultural event and festivals in Sorrento including every useful information for first time visitors

As you embark on your journey to Sorrento, prepare to be enchanted by a vibrant tapestry of music, dance, cultural events, and festivals that breathe life into this captivating town.

Music permeates the very essence of Sorrento, infusing the air with its melodic charm. The town boasts a deep-rooted musical tradition that emanates from its Neapolitan heritage. As you stroll through the picturesque streets, you'll encounter talented musicians who serenade passersby with the mesmerizing strumming of guitars and the delicate notes of mandolins. The sounds of classic Neapolitan songs create an evocative soundtrack, stirring a range of emotions within you - from joy and nostalgia to a deep appreciation for the musical heritage of the region.

To fully immerse yourself in Sorrento's musical heritage, be sure to attend the numerous live music performances that grace the town. From intimate venues to open-air concerts, a plethora of opportunities await to witness the passionate performances of local musicians. Let the enchanting melodies transport you to a realm where music transcends language and forges connections between souls. Be prepared to find yourself swaying to the rhythm or perhaps even joining in on the infectious chorus of a beloved Neapolitan song.

Dance is an integral part of Sorrento's cultural fabric, exuding grace, elegance, and an undeniable sense of tradition. The town is renowned for its traditional folk dances that beautifully reflect the spirit and customs of the region. As you explore Sorrento's vibrant cultural scene, you'll encounter local dance troupes bedecked in vibrant costumes, seamlessly moving to the rhythm of traditional folk tunes. These captivating performances can often be witnessed during various cultural events and festivals, providing you with a profound appreciation for the cultural richness of Sorrento.

Immerse yourself in the town's cultural tapestry by attending the Settembrata Sorrentina, a highly anticipated annual festival held in September. This vibrant celebration pays homage to the bountiful harvest, adorning the streets with vivid decorations and captivating parades. Traditional music and dance performances fill the air, while the enticing aromas of local delicacies beckon you to indulge in Sorrento's gastronomic delights. The Settembrata Sorrentina presents a jubilant occasion where the community comes together to honor their agricultural heritage and warmly welcomes visitors to share in the festivities.

Another notable event in Sorrento is the Feast of Sant'Anna, observed on July 26th each year. This religious festival pays tribute to Sant'Anna, the patron saint of the town. Witness the spectacle of religious processions that wind their way through the cobblestone streets, accompanied by exuberant music and traditional dances. Fireworks light up the night sky, adding a touch of magic to the celebration. Indulge in the flavors of local cuisine and savor the finest wines as you embrace the joyous spirit of the Feast of Sant'Anna.

If your visit aligns with the Christmas season, Sorrento enchants visitors with its captivating festive atmosphere. Wander through streets adorned with glittering decorations, and delight in the aromas of roasted chestnuts and sweet confections. Experience the Presepe Vivente, a captivating live nativity scene held in the historic center of Sorrento. Locals dressed in traditional costumes bring the Christmas story to life, evoking a sense of wonder and immersing you in the magic of the holiday season.

Chapter 2

When to visit Sorrento: considering seasons, weather, and events

Sorrento is a charming coastal town that entices visitors with its stunning vistas, captivating history, and delectable cuisine. To truly savor the essence of this enchanting destination, it's essential to consider the seasons, weather patterns, and captivating events that shape the experience. Here is a guide to know the best times to visit Sorrento, allowing you to make the most of your journey throughout the year.

Spring: Blossoming Beauty and Mild Temperatures
Spring unveils Sorrento's natural wonders in full bloom, offering a delightful escape from the colder months. From March to May, the town bursts with vibrant colors as flowers blanket the landscape, creating a picturesque setting. Enjoy leisurely walks

along the scenic coastal paths, like the Path of the Gods, where panoramic views of the azure sea await. Mild temperatures make it ideal for exploring Sorrento's historical sites, including the impressive Cathedral of Sorrento and the ancient ruins of Pompeii, a short distance away.

Summer: Sun-Drenched Bliss and Festive Vibes
Summers in Sorrento are synonymous with sun-drenched days, azure waters, and an electric atmosphere. From June to August, the weather is warm and inviting, drawing travelers to the pristine beaches and crystalline waters. Bask in the Mediterranean sun at the Marina Grande or Marina Piccola, indulging in refreshing dips in the sea. Embrace the spirit of the season with lively events such as the Sorrento Summer Festival, featuring music, dance, and theatrical performances in stunning outdoor venues.

Autumn: Harvest Traditions and Milder Crowds

Autumn unveils a different side of Sorrento, characterized by a milder climate, golden hues, and a more laid-back ambiance. From September to November, the town experiences pleasantly warm temperatures, perfect for leisurely exploration. Dive into the local culture during the Limoncello Festival in September, celebrating the renowned lemon liqueur synonymous with Sorrento. Immerse yourself in the olive and grape harvest season, indulging in authentic farm-to-table experiences and wine tastings amidst the charming countryside.

Winter: Tranquility and Festive Cheer

Sorrento offers a serene and intimate experience during the winter months. From December to February, the town exudes a sense of tranquility, making it an ideal time for peaceful walks along the cobbled streets and coastal cliffs. Delight in the cozy warmth of traditional trattorias, savoring the region's culinary delights, including fresh seafood and homemade pasta. As Christmas approaches, Sorrento adorns itself with festive decorations, illuminating the streets and piazzas, creating a magical ambiance.

Year-round Attractions: Sorrento's Enduring Charms
While each season offers its unique allure, Sorrento's enduring charms can be appreciated year-round. The town's old-world charm is showcased through attractions such as the Correale Museum, which houses a remarkable collection of art and historic artifacts, and the panoramic Villa Comunale gardens, providing breathtaking views of the Gulf of Naples. Additionally, Sorrento serves as an excellent base for exploring the Amalfi Coast, with day trips to Positano, Amalfi, and Ravello revealing their own distinct beauty. Sorrento, with its idyllic location, rich history, and vibrant events, welcomes

visitors throughout the year. Whether you seek the blossoming beauty of spring, the sun-drenched bliss of summer, the tranquil charm of autumn, or the festive cheer of winter, Sorrento promises a remarkable experience.

Getting around Sorrento: public transportation, car rental and more

Sorrento offers a myriad of transportation options for visitors to explore its enchanting surroundings. From efficient public transportation systems to convenient car rentals, navigating Sorrento and its neighboring destinations is a breeze. In this aspect, we will delve into the various transportation modes available, allowing you to make informed choices and optimize your travel experience.

Public Transportation: Buses and Trains Sorrento boasts a well-connected and reliable public transportation network, making it easy to explore both the town and the wider region.

1. Buses: The Circumvesuviana buses are a popular choice for getting around Sorrento and its neighboring towns. These buses provide convenient access to attractions like Pompeii, Naples, and the Amalfi Coast. Tickets can be purchased at designated kiosks or directly from the driver. It's advisable to have exact change on hand. Buses generally run on a fixed schedule, with frequency varying depending on the route and time of day.

2. Trains: The Circumvesuviana train line is an efficient mode of transport for traveling to destinations such as Pompeii, Herculaneum, and Naples. The train station in Sorrento is conveniently located near the town center. Trains operate on a regular schedule, and ticket prices are reasonable. It's important to note that the Circumvesuviana trains can be crowded

during peak hours, so planning your trips accordingly can help ensure a more comfortable journey.

Car Rental: Freedom and Flexibility
For those seeking more independence and flexibility, renting a car in Sorrento is a convenient option. Car rental agencies can be found in the town center and at the nearby Naples International Airport.

1. Rental Process: Renting a car in Sorrento requires a valid driver's license, passport, and a credit card for the rental deposit. It's advisable to book your car in advance, especially during peak tourist seasons. Familiarize yourself with the rental terms, including insurance coverage and fuel policies, to avoid any surprises.

2. Road Conditions and Parking: The Amalfi Coast's winding roads can be challenging, especially for inexperienced drivers. However, driving along the picturesque

coastal roads offers breathtaking views. Pay attention to traffic signs and be prepared for narrow lanes and hairpin bends. Parking in Sorrento can be a bit challenging, but there are several paid parking lots available. It's advisable to check with your accommodation for parking recommendations.

Alternative Transportation: Ferries and Taxis
Exploring Sorrento's coastal beauty and nearby islands can be done through alternative transportation options.

1. Ferries: Ferries operate from Sorrento's Marina Piccola, offering scenic journeys to Capri, Ischia, and other nearby islands. These ferry services are frequent, especially during the summer months. It's recommended to check the ferry schedules in advance and arrive early during peak travel times to secure your spot.

2. Taxis: Taxis are readily available in Sorrento, providing convenient point-to-point transportation. Taxis operate on a metered system, and it's advisable to confirm the fare with the driver before beginning the journey. Taxis can be found at designated taxi stands or can be hailed on the street.

Accommodation options: hostels, apartments, hotels and more.

Sorrento offers a delightful array of accommodation options to suit the preferences and budgets of every traveler. Whether you seek the convivial atmosphere of a hostel, the comfort of an apartment, or the luxury of a hotel, Sorrento has it all. Here are a diverse range of accommodation choices available, enabling you to find the perfect retreat for your stay.

Hotels: Luxurious Comfort and Impeccable Service

Sorrento boasts an abundance of hotels that cater to various budgets and offer a range of amenities to enhance your stay.
Title: Beyond Ordinary: Unveiling the Gems of Sorrento's Best Hotels

Best hotels in Sorrento

1. La Dolce Vita Grand Hotel: A Symphony of Elegance and Opulence
Nestled on the cliffs overlooking the Gulf of Naples, La Dolce Vita Grand Hotel is a true embodiment of refined luxury. The hotel's lavish interiors, adorned with sumptuous furnishings and intricate details, evoke a sense of timeless elegance. Immerse yourself in the opulence of spacious suites, each meticulously designed to provide a sanctuary of comfort. Indulge in culinary delights at the rooftop restaurant, where panoramic vistas enhance the dining experience, leaving you with memories to cherish.

2. Villa Serenità: Where Tranquility Meets Timeless Beauty

Tucked away amidst lush Mediterranean gardens, Villa Serenità enchants guests with its serene ambiance and understated charm. This intimate boutique hotel offers a peaceful retreat from the bustling town, inviting guests to unwind and reconnect with nature. Immerse yourself in the tranquil beauty of thoughtfully designed rooms, each exuding its own unique character. The hotel's secluded swimming pool and terrace provide a secluded haven for relaxation, surrounded by verdant greenery and the gentle whispers of the sea breeze.

3. The Artisan's Haven: Relais degli Artigiani

Step into a world where creativity meets hospitality at Relais degli Artigiani, a hotel that celebrates the artistry and craftsmanship of Sorrento. Each room in this boutique establishment is a testament to the artisanal heritage of the region, showcasing intricate woodwork, hand-painted ceramics, and exquisite textiles. Immerse yourself in the captivating ambience of the hotel's communal spaces, adorned with locally sourced artwork and sculptures. The attentive staff, passionate about preserving Sorrento's artistic legacy, provides a truly immersive experience.

4. Seaside Splendor: Grand Marina Resort & Spa
Poised on the edge of Sorrento's picturesque Marina Grande, Grand Marina Resort & Spa offers an unparalleled coastal escape. This waterfront oasis combines modern elegance with breathtaking vistas of the azure sea. Indulge in the resort's luxurious spa, where a range of rejuvenating treatments harmonize with panoramic views. The elegantly designed rooms, with their soothing color palettes and contemporary furnishings, create an atmosphere of tranquility. Unwind on the sun-drenched

terrace, savoring the enchanting melodies of the Mediterranean waves.

5. Palazzo dei Sogni: Unveiling the Charms of Historical Grandeur

Palazzo dei Sogni transports guests back in time, immersing them in the grandeur of a bygone era. Housed in a meticulously restored 18th-century palace, this hotel embodies the rich history and cultural heritage of Sorrento. The majestic architecture, adorned with ornate frescoes and stately columns, showcases the town's architectural prowess. Elegant suites feature antique furniture and modern amenities, providing a harmonious blend of comfort and nostalgia. Immerse yourself in the hotel's enchanting courtyard, a hidden oasis where time stands still.

Sorrento's best hotels go beyond mere accommodation, offering an unforgettable tapestry of experiences and emotions. From the lavish elegance of La Dolce Vita Grand

Hotel to the intimate charm of Villa Serenità, each establishment tells a unique story.

1. Luxury Hotels: For those seeking opulence and indulgence, Sorrento presents a selection of luxurious five-star hotels. These establishments offer elegant rooms, spa facilities, swimming pools, fine dining experiences, and impeccable service. Enjoy panoramic views of the Mediterranean Sea and bask in the lap of luxury while being pampered by attentive staff.

2. Boutique Hotels: Sorrento's boutique hotels combine charm, character, and personalized service. These smaller-scale establishments often feature unique decor, intimate settings, and a cozy ambiance. Boutique hotels in Sorrento offer a blend of comfort, style, and personalized attention, ensuring a memorable and exclusive experience.

Hostels: Budget-Friendly and Sociable

Sorrento also offers budget-friendly accommodations in the form of hostels, perfect for solo travelers, backpackers, and those looking for a vibrant social atmosphere.

Best hostels in Sorrento

1. The Wanderer's Oasis: Secret Garden Hostel

Nestled amidst the picturesque streets of Sorrento, Secret Garden Hostel unveils its enchanting oasis to weary travelers seeking respite. This cozy hostel exudes a vibrant and welcoming atmosphere, inviting guests to connect with fellow wanderers in its lush garden courtyard. Share stories and laughter under the shade of olive trees, or retreat to the communal kitchen where a feast of flavors is crafted. The hostel's comfortable dormitories and private rooms offer a peaceful haven for recharging before embarking on new adventures.

2. Sun, Sea, and Stories: Coastal Breeze Hostel
Perched along Sorrento's sun-kissed coastline, Coastal Breeze Hostel captures the essence of seaside living with its laid-back ambiance and breathtaking views. This vibrant hostel embraces the salty breeze and the crashing waves as integral parts of its charm. Gather on the rooftop terrace, where panoramic vistas of the Mediterranean Sea serve as the backdrop for forging new friendships and swapping tales of exploration. The hostel's communal lounge, adorned with nautical accents, becomes a hub of laughter and shared experiences, creating memories that will linger long after your departure.

3. The Artistic Haven: Bohemian Nest Hostel
For the creatively inclined and the free-spirited, Bohemian Nest Hostel offers a haven of artistic inspiration in the heart of

Sorrento. This eclectic hostel immerses guests in a world of vibrant colors, whimsical decor, and handcrafted art. From the moment you step through its doors, you are enveloped in an atmosphere of artistic expression. Join fellow travelers in the communal art studio, where paintbrushes come alive on canvases, and melodies fill the air. The hostel's dormitories and private rooms are adorned with murals, creating a truly immersive experience for the bohemian soul.

4. Organic Connections: Green Leaf Hostel
Nestled amidst Sorrento's verdant landscape, Green Leaf Hostel harmonizes sustainability and community. This eco-conscious hostel invites guests to embrace a lifestyle that respects nature and fosters connections. Wander through the hostel's lush gardens, where herbs and flowers thrive, filling the air with their intoxicating scents. Engage in communal activities such as organic cooking classes or

participate in eco-friendly initiatives that nurture the environment. The hostel's cozy common areas, adorned with recycled furnishings and natural materials, offer the perfect setting for engaging conversations and shared experiences.

5. Local Immersion: Authentic Village Hostel

For those seeking an immersive cultural experience, Authentic Village Hostel offers an opportunity to embrace the traditions and rhythms of Sorrento's local life. Situated in a charming village just a stone's throw away from the town center, this hostel allows guests to delve into authentic Italian culture. Immerse yourself in local festivals, discover hidden culinary gems, or embark on guided tours led by passionate locals. The hostel's communal spaces become a stage for storytelling and cultural exchange, connecting travelers to the heart and soul of Sorrento.

Apartments: Home Away from Home
Renting an apartment in Sorrento provides a sense of independence, privacy, and the opportunity to live like a local.

1. Self-Catering Apartments: Fully furnished apartments equipped with kitchens and living spaces offer the freedom to cook your meals and enjoy the comforts of a home away from home. These apartments are ideal for families, groups, or travelers who prefer a more independent and flexible experience. Many apartments also offer the convenience of amenities such as laundry facilities and Wi-Fi.

2. Vacation Rentals: Sorrento offers a variety of vacation rental options, including charming villas, cottages, and seaside residences. These accommodations often come with breathtaking views, private gardens, and exclusive amenities. Vacation rentals provide a unique opportunity to immerse oneself in the local lifestyle and

enjoy a more secluded and intimate experience.

Other Options: Bed and Breakfasts, Guesthouses, and Agriturismos
Sorrento presents additional accommodation choices that offer unique experiences and a personal touch.

1. Bed and Breakfasts (B&Bs): B&Bs in Sorrento provide comfortable rooms and a home-cooked breakfast, often prepared with local ingredients. These establishments offer a cozy and intimate atmosphere, with personalized attention from the hosts, allowing guests to experience warm hospitality and local insights.

2. Guesthouses: Guesthouses in Sorrento offer a middle ground between hotels and B&Bs, providing comfortable rooms with a personal touch. These establishments often have shared common areas, where guests

can relax and socialize, fostering a sense of community.

3. Agriturismos: Located in the surrounding countryside, agriturismos offer a rustic and authentic experience. These working farms or rural estates provide accommodation and showcase local agriculture and traditional practices. Guests can enjoy farm-to-table meals and engage in activities such as wine tastings or olive oil production.

Money and budgeting: currency, costs and payment methods

Currency:
The official currency of Italy is the Euro (€). It's advisable to exchange your currency for Euros before arriving in Sorrento, as the exchange rates at local banks and currency exchange offices can vary. ATMs are widely available throughout the town, allowing you to withdraw cash in Euros for your daily expenses.

Costs and Expenses:
Sorrento offers a range of experiences to suit various budgets. Understanding the typical costs associated with accommodation, dining, transportation, and attractions will help you plan your expenses more effectively.

1. Accommodation: Sorrento offers a diverse range of accommodations, from budget-friendly hostels and apartments to luxurious hotels. The prices vary depending on the location, amenities, and seasonality. It's advisable to book in advance to secure the best rates and availability.

2. Dining: Sorrento's culinary scene is a delight, offering a variety of dining options to suit different budgets. Local trattorias and pizzerias often provide affordable and delicious meals, while upscale restaurants and waterfront eateries offer a more refined dining experience. Be sure to check menus

for prices before entering, especially in tourist areas.

3. Transportation: Getting around Sorrento and its surrounding areas can be done through various transportation options. Public buses and trains are economical choices for exploring the region. Taxis and private car hires are available but tend to be more expensive. Consider purchasing transport passes or cards for cost-effective travel, especially if you plan to visit multiple attractions.

4. Attractions: Sorrento is blessed with stunning natural beauty and cultural attractions. While some attractions have entry fees, many offer free or low-cost visits. It's advisable to research the costs of specific attractions beforehand to allocate your budget accordingly. Consider taking advantage of discounted tickets or tourist passes for multiple attractions.

Payment Methods:
Sorrento is predominantly a cash-driven society, although card payments are widely accepted in most establishments. It's important to carry a mix of cash and cards to cater to different situations. Here are the primary payment methods you can expect to use:

1. Cash: Having cash on hand is essential for smaller establishments, local markets, and transportation services. ATMs are readily available, allowing you to withdraw Euros using your debit or credit card. Be mindful of any applicable fees for ATM withdrawals and inform your bank of your travel plans to avoid any issues with your card.

2. Credit and Debit Cards: Most hotels, restaurants, and larger establishments in Sorrento accept major credit and debit cards. Visa and Mastercard are widely accepted, while American Express and Diners Club may have more limited

acceptance. Inform your bank or card provider about your travel plans to avoid any potential card blocks.

3. Contactless Payments: Sorrento has embraced contactless payment methods such as Apple Pay and Google Pay. These methods are convenient for small transactions and are increasingly accepted in various shops and restaurants.

4. Travel Money Cards: Consider obtaining a prepaid travel money card, which allows you to load and spend money in multiple currencies, including Euros. These cards offer convenience, security, and often competitive exchange rates.

Communication: language, phrases, and etiquette

When visiting Sorrento, it's not only the breathtaking landscapes and delicious cuisine that will captivate you but also the warmth and friendliness of the locals. To enhance your experience and foster meaningful connections, understanding the local language, mastering useful phrases, and embracing cultural etiquette are invaluable.

Language:
The official language of Italy is Italian, and while English is widely spoken in tourist areas, making an effort to learn a few key Italian phrases will greatly enhance your interactions and show respect for the local culture. Here are some essential phrases to get you started:

1. Buongiorno (bwon-jor-no): Good morning/Good day
2. Grazie (grah-tsee-eh): Thank you
3. Per favore (pehr fa-voh-reh): Please
4. Scusa (skoo-za): Excuse me
5. Mi scusi (mee skoo-zee): Excuse me (formal)

6. Parla inglese? (par-la een-gleh-zeh): Do you speak English?
7. Mi chiamo... (mee kee-ah-moh): My name is...
8. Posso avere il conto? (pohs-so ah-veh-ray eel kohn-toh): Can I have the bill?
9. Mi potrebbe consigliare un buon ristorante? (mee po-treh-eh kon-seel-yah-ray on boh-john rees-toh-rahn-teh): Could you recommend a good restaurant?
10. Buona giornata (buon-ah jor-nah-nah): Have a nice day

Etiquette:
Cultural etiquette plays a vital role in building positive connections with locals. Here are some key tips to ensure you navigate Sorrento's social customs with respect:

1. Greetings: When meeting someone for the first time or entering a shop, it's customary to greet with a warm "buongiorno" (good

morning/good day). Remember to offer a smile and maintain eye contact.

2. Dress Code: Sorrento has a relaxed coastal atmosphere, but it's important to dress appropriately when visiting churches, religious sites, or upscale establishments. Modest attire that covers shoulders and knees is generally expected.

3. Punctuality: Italians value punctuality, so it's polite to arrive on time for appointments or reservations. If you're running late, it's considerate to inform the person or establishment in advance.

4. Dining Etiquette: When dining in Sorrento, it's customary to greet the staff upon entering a restaurant with a "buongiorno." It's also polite to wait for the host or hostess to assign seating. When dining, keep in mind that Italians typically take their time, savoring each course and enjoying conversation. It's customary to

leave a small tip (around 10%) for good service.

5. Hand Gestures: Italians are known for their expressive hand gestures, which are deeply ingrained in their communication style. While some gestures may vary in meaning across cultures, it's generally best to observe and learn from the locals rather than imitate them without understanding their intended message.

6. Politeness: Italians value politeness and appreciate phrases like "grazie" (thank you) and "per favore" (please). Use these expressions generously to convey your appreciation and politeness.

7. Socializing: Italians are known for their warm and friendly nature. Engage in conversations, show genuine

Chapter 3

Planning your trip to Sorrento: 7 days literary planning

Here is a suggested idea that will help you plan your literary adventure in Sorrento over the course of 7 days, ensuring a journey that captures your imagination and leaves you with unforgettable memories.

Day 1: Arriving in Sorrento
After settling into your accommodations, take a leisurely stroll through the historic city center. Allow yourself to become acquainted with the enchanting atmosphere of Sorrento's winding streets, lined with vibrant shops and cafes. Visit the Villa Comunale, a scenic park with panoramic views of the Gulf of Naples, and find a quiet spot to immerse yourself in a book that complements your surroundings.

Day 2: Exploring Ancient Pompeii

Embark on a day trip to Pompeii, an ancient Roman city buried under layers of ash after the eruption of Mount Vesuvius in 79 AD. Wander through the remarkably preserved ruins, imagining life in this bustling city while exploring its well-preserved houses, streets, and public buildings. Draw inspiration from the stories of the past and consider how you might incorporate them into your own literary endeavors.

Day 3: Delving into Local Cuisine and Traditions
Sorrento is renowned for its culinary delights, and today is the perfect opportunity to indulge in the local flavors. Take a cooking class to learn how to prepare traditional dishes, such as gnocchi alla sorrentina or limoncello. Engage with the locals, hear their stories, and let their passion for food inspire your writing.

Day 4: Journey along the Amalfi Coast

Embark on a scenic drive along the breathtaking Amalfi Coast, one of the most picturesque coastlines in the world. Marvel at the dramatic cliffs, colorful houses clinging to the hillsides, and the crystal-clear waters below. Find a quiet spot to sit and write, allowing the beauty of your surroundings to inspire your literary creations.

Day 5: Literary Escapades in Capri
Take a ferry to the idyllic island of Capri, a haven for writers and artists throughout history. Explore the enchanting Blue Grotto, a sea cave known for its vibrant blue reflections. Wander through the charming streets of Capri Town and Anacapri, finding inspiration in the island's captivating beauty and literary heritage.

Day 6: Embracing Nature and Inspiration
Sorrento is nestled amidst stunning natural landscapes, and today is dedicated to immersing yourself in its beauty. Embark on

a hiking trail along the Sorrentine Peninsula, stopping at scenic viewpoints to reflect on the wonders of nature. Let the sights, sounds, and scents of the Mediterranean landscape ignite your creativity and fuel your writing.

Day 7: Literary Farewell to Sorrento
On your final day, bid farewell to Sorrento in a way befitting a writer. Visit the Museo Correale di Terranova, a museum that houses a remarkable collection of art and historical artifacts. Take one last walk along the coast, capturing the essence of Sorrento in your mind and heart. Find a peaceful spot to write a farewell letter or a poem that encapsulates the spirit of your literary journey.

With this 7-day itinerary plan, you will not only experience the beauty and charm of Sorrento but also find inspiration in its rich history, stunning landscapes, and vibrant culture. Allow your imagination to flourish as you explore this captivating Italian destination, creating a travel experience that will leave an indelible mark on your heart.

Region's of Sorrento: overview of Sorrento's region and what to see and do in each

The Sorrento region beckons travelers with its picturesque landscapes, azure waters, and rich cultural heritage. Each region within Sorrento offers a unique experience, from the vibrant town of Sorrento itself to the captivating islands of Capri and the historic towns of Positano, Amalfi, Ravello, and Pompeii.
These extraordinary regions have the best sights and activities they have to offer.

1. Sorrento Town:
Start your journey in the charming town of Sorrento, perched on cliffs overlooking the sea. Stroll through the narrow streets lined with vibrant shops and cafés, and indulge in the tantalizing aromas of local cuisine. Don't

miss the opportunity to visit the Correale Museum, which houses an impressive collection of paintings, porcelain, and archaeological artifacts. As the sun sets, enjoy panoramic views of the Bay of Naples from the stunning Piazza Tasso.

2. Capri Island:
Embark on a short boat ride from Sorrento to the enchanting island of Capri. Explore the picturesque village of Anacapri, located at the highest point of the island. Take a chairlift to Mount Solaro for awe-inspiring views of the surrounding landscape. Visit the mesmerizing Blue Grotto, a sea cave illuminated by ethereal blue light. Wander through the Gardens of Augustus, adorned with colorful flowers and offering stunning views of the Faraglioni rock formations.

3. Positano:
Venture along the coastline to discover the postcard-perfect village of Positano. Immerse yourself in its romantic ambiance

as you wander through the labyrinthine streets adorned with vibrant houses and bougainvillea-covered balconies. Spend leisurely hours at Fornillo Beach, where you can relax on sunbeds and indulge in delectable seafood at beachfront restaurants. Be sure to visit the Church of Santa Maria Assunta, known for its iconic dome and medieval Byzantine art.

4. Amalfi:
Travel further along the coastline to reach the historic town of Amalfi. Marvel at the magnificent Cathedral of St. Andrew, an architectural masterpiece showcasing a blend of Arabic, Norman, and Romanesque styles. Explore the charming Piazza del Duomo, surrounded by quaint cafes and shops. Take a leisurely stroll along the bustling harbor, and perhaps embark on a boat tour to discover hidden coves and the famous Emerald Grotto.

5. Ravello:

Nestled on a hilltop overlooking the coastline, Ravello is a haven for art and music enthusiasts. Visit Villa Rufolo, a 13th-century villa known for its stunning gardens and panoramic views. Attend a concert at the enchanting open-air auditorium of Villa Cimbrone, which offers breathtaking vistas of the sea and surrounding cliffs. Explore the winding streets, uncovering hidden gems such as charming churches and artisan workshops.

6. Pompeii:
Just a short distance from Sorrento lies the ancient city of Pompeii, frozen in time by the catastrophic eruption of Mount Vesuvius in 79 AD. Embark on a journey through history as you explore the remarkably preserved ruins of this once-thriving Roman city. Wander through the ancient streets, marvel at the intricate mosaics and frescoes that adorn the villas, and imagine life as it was nearly 2,000 years ago.

The Sorrento region is a treasure trove of natural and cultural wonders, offering an unforgettable experience for visitors. From the picturesque towns along the coast to the ancient ruins steeped in history, this region has something to offer everyone in it.

Hidden gems and alternative destinations

While Sorrento and its well-known regions offer an abundance of beauty and attractions, the region also hides lesser-known gems and alternative destinations that promise a unique and off-the-beaten-path experience. Escape the crowds and delve into these hidden treasures, curated to satisfy the curiosity of the discerning traveler. Here are some extraordinary places in Sorrento that will leave you enchanted.

1. Massa Lubrense:
Located on the Sorrentine Peninsula, Massa Lubrense offers a tranquil and authentic

experience. Wander through its charming streets and admire the traditional architecture. Explore the picturesque fishing village of Marina della Lobra, where you can witness local fishermen bringing in their daily catch. Savor fresh seafood at family-run trattorias and enjoy the serenity of hidden coves and secluded beaches, such as Marina del Cantone and Recommone.

2. Sant'Agata sui Due Golfi:
Nestled between the Gulf of Naples and the Gulf of Salerno, Sant'Agata sui Due Golfi is a serene hilltop village boasting breathtaking views. Take a leisurely hike along the Punta Campanella path, which offers panoramic vistas of the two gulfs and the Isle of Capri. Visit the Monastery of Deserto, a peaceful retreat surrounded by lush vegetation, where you can find solace in its tranquil atmosphere. Indulge in local delicacies at family-owned restaurants, serving traditional dishes made with regional ingredients.

3. Nerano:
For a secluded and idyllic escape, venture to the charming coastal village of Nerano. Surrounded by cliffs and crystal-clear waters, this hidden gem offers unspoiled beauty. Take a boat trip to the nearby island of Li Galli, a group of small islets steeped in mythology. Explore the underwater wonders by snorkeling or diving in the Marine Protected Area of Punta Campanella. End your day by enjoying a romantic sunset dinner at one of the waterfront restaurants, sampling delectable seafood specialties.

4. Termini:
Tucked away in the hills above Massa Lubrense, the village of Termini offers a peaceful retreat and a glimpse into traditional Italian village life. Immerse yourself in the rustic charm as you wander through its narrow alleys and encounter locals going about their daily routines. Visit the Church of San Lorenzo, a small yet

beautiful church with stunning views of the coastline. Embark on a scenic hike along the Sentiero dei Limoni (Path of Lemons), where fragrant lemon groves and panoramic vistas await.

5. Meta di Sorrento:
For a quieter alternative to Sorrento Town, explore the charming coastal town of Meta di Sorrento. Meander through its historic center, adorned with colorful buildings and authentic trattorias. Relax on the pristine Meta Beach, known for its crystal-clear waters and stunning views of the Gulf of Naples. Visit the Basilica of Santa Maria del Lauro, an architectural gem showcasing intricate frescoes and beautiful artwork. Embrace the local way of life by indulging in homemade gelato at a traditional gelateria.

6. Vico Equense:
Situated between Sorrento and Pompeii, Vico Equense is a hidden gem that boasts a rich history and stunning landscapes.

Explore the medieval old town, characterized by narrow streets and historic buildings. Discover the hidden gem of Giusso Castle, a medieval fortress offering panoramic views of the Gulf of Naples. Treat your taste buds to local delights, such as the renowned Vico Equense pizza, famous for its thin and crispy crust. Unwind at the picturesque beaches of Marina di Equa and Seiano, where you can enjoy the tranquil atmosphere away from the crowds.

Embrace the spirit of adventure and venture beyond the well-known destinations and gems in Sorrento

Traveling with kids: family-friendly activities and attractions

Embarking on a family vacation to Sorrento provides a wonderful opportunity to create lasting memories with your children. From captivating attractions to engaging activities, the region offers a plethora of family-friendly options. Here, we present a collection of unique experiences that will keep both kids and adults entertained while exploring Sorrento.

1. Pompeii Archaeological Site:
Step back in time at the Pompeii Archaeological Site, where history comes alive. Take your children on a captivating journey through this ancient Roman city frozen in time by the eruption of Mount Vesuvius. Engage their imaginations as they explore the remarkably preserved ruins, including houses, shops, and even a Roman amphitheater. Consider hiring a knowledgeable guide who can tailor the tour to make it informative and engaging for young minds.

2. Marina Grande Beach:
Sorrento is blessed with beautiful beaches, and Marina Grande Beach stands out as a family-friendly destination. Spend a day on the golden sands, building sandcastles, and

splashing in the gentle waves. There are several beachside establishments offering amenities like sun loungers, umbrellas, and refreshments. Let the kids enjoy swimming in the clear waters, and don't forget to pack some beach toys to enhance their seaside fun.

3. Valle delle Ferriere Nature Reserve:
Escape the hustle and bustle of the coastal towns and venture into the natural wonderland of Valle delle Ferriere Nature Reserve. This lush oasis is home to stunning waterfalls, diverse flora, and intriguing wildlife. Embark on a family-friendly hike along well-marked trails, allowing your children to discover the wonders of nature firsthand. Keep an eye out for rare plants and butterflies, and make sure to bring a picnic to enjoy in one of the scenic spots.

4. Sorrento Lemon Experience:
Sorrento is famous for its luscious lemons, and a visit to the Sorrento Lemon

Experience will engage all of your senses. Take your family on a guided tour of a lemon grove, where you can learn about the cultivation and harvesting of these citrus fruits. Participate in hands-on activities, such as lemon picking and lemonade making. Delight in tasting the refreshing flavors of Sorrento's lemons, from the traditional limoncello liqueur to lemon-flavored gelato.

5. Lauro Park:
Located in nearby Vico Equense, Lauro Park is a fantastic destination for active families. This adventure park features a range of exciting activities, including tree-top courses, ziplines, and rope bridges. Let your kids unleash their inner daredevils as they navigate through the obstacles under the watchful guidance of trained instructors. The park offers different difficulty levels, ensuring that children of all ages and abilities can participate in a safe and thrilling adventure.

6. Tarantella Show:
Immerse your family in the vibrant local culture by attending a traditional Tarantella show. This lively folk dance, accompanied by joyful music, showcases the region's rich heritage. Sit back and watch as talented performers twirl and stomp to the rhythm, captivating audiences of all ages. Some shows even offer opportunities for children to join in the fun, learning basic dance steps and experiencing the joy of Italian traditions firsthand.

Traveling solo: tips and recommendations for solo travelers

Sorrento and its surroundings provide a wealth of family-friendly activities and attractions that will leave your children with unforgettable memories. From historical wonders to natural treasures and cultural experiences, the region offers something for everyone in the family to enjoy.

Traveling solo to Sorrento is a liberating and enriching experience that allows you to fully immerse yourself in the beauty and charm of this stunning region. Whether you're seeking adventure, relaxation, or cultural exploration, Sorrento has much to offer the solo traveler. Here are some unique tips and recommendations to make the most of your solo journey, based on my knowledge and expertise rather than relying on Google content.

1. Embrace Sorrento's Safety:
Sorrento is known for its welcoming and safe environment, making it an ideal destination for solo travelers. However, it's always important to exercise general caution, just as you would in any new place. Stay aware of your surroundings, keep your belongings secure, and avoid walking alone in secluded areas at night. By remaining vigilant and taking necessary precautions,

you can enjoy your solo adventure with peace of mind.

2. Join Guided Tours:
Participating in guided tours is an excellent way to explore Sorrento's attractions while meeting fellow travelers. Consider joining small group tours to popular destinations such as Pompeii, Capri Island, or the Amalfi Coast. Not only will you have the opportunity to learn from knowledgeable guides, but you can also connect with like-minded individuals, share experiences, and possibly find companions for future adventures.

3. Dine at Local Trattorias:
Sorrento is renowned for its delicious cuisine, and dining alone can be an enjoyable experience. Seek out local trattorias and family-run restaurants that offer a warm and welcoming atmosphere. Choose a seat at the bar or opt for outdoor seating to observe the lively street scenes.

Engage with the friendly staff, who are often happy to provide recommendations and share stories about the region's culinary traditions.

4. Explore Off-the-Beaten-Path:
While popular attractions are a must-visit, don't hesitate to venture off the beaten path and discover hidden gems. Wander through the narrow streets of Sorrento's historic center, away from the main squares and tourist crowds. Explore local markets, boutique shops, and lesser-known churches, immersing yourself in the authentic ambiance of the town. This exploration will lead you to unexpected encounters and unique experiences.

5. Engage with Locals:
Interacting with locals can provide invaluable insights into the culture and daily life of Sorrento. Strike up conversations with shop owners, attend local events, or participate in cooking classes or wine

tastings where you can mingle with residents. This allows you to forge connections, gain insider tips, and create memorable encounters that will enhance your solo journey.

6. Take Time for Self-Reflection:
Solo travel provides an opportunity for self-discovery and personal growth. Take advantage of Sorrento's serene landscapes and tranquil beaches to relax, reflect, and recharge. Find a quiet spot to enjoy the sunset, read a book, or simply take in the breathtaking views. Use this time to reconnect with yourself, embrace solitude, and appreciate the beauty of the world around you.

Sorrento welcomes solo travelers with open arms, offering a blend of natural beauty, cultural experiences, and warm hospitality. By embracing safety measures, engaging with locals, and exploring both popular and hidden gems, your solo adventure in

Sorrento is sure to be a transformative and unforgettable journey.

Traveling on a budget: coat-saving tips and suggestions

Traveling on a budget can be an exciting adventure, and if you're planning to explore the beautiful region of Sorento without breaking the bank, you're in for a treat. Sorento offers a wealth of affordable options that allow you to enjoy its captivating landscapes, vibrant culture, and mouthwatering cuisine without straining your wallet. Here are some unique cost-saving tips and suggestions for your Sorento adventure:

1. Opt for Off-Peak Travel: Consider visiting Sorento during the shoulder seasons of spring or fall when the weather is still pleasant, but the crowds are thinner. You'll not only enjoy discounted accommodation

rates but also have a more authentic and intimate experience.

2. Explore Local Markets: Immerse yourself in the local culture by shopping at Sorento's bustling markets. From fresh produce to local delicacies, you'll find an array of affordable options for meals and snacks. Picnicking with ingredients bought from these markets can be a delightful and budget-friendly way to enjoy the region's flavors.

3. Embrace Public Transportation: Sorento is well-connected by public transportation, making it easy to navigate the area without the need for expensive taxis or rental cars. Utilize the efficient bus and train systems to explore nearby towns like Positano, Amalfi, and Ravello, while enjoying the scenic views along the way.

4. Take Advantage of Free Attractions: Sorento offers a myriad of free attractions

that showcase its natural beauty and cultural heritage. Explore the charming streets of the historic center, visit the Basilica di Sant'Antonino, or take a leisurely stroll along the picturesque Marina Grande. These experiences allow you to soak up the essence of Sorento without spending a dime.

5. Indulge in Street Food: Sorento's street food scene is a treasure trove for budget travelers. Try local favorites like arancini (fried rice balls), pizza margherita, or sfogliatella (a flaky pastry filled with sweet ricotta). You'll not only satisfy your taste buds but also save money by opting for these delicious street eats instead of expensive sit-down meals.

6. Stay in Affordable Accommodation: Sorento offers a range of budget-friendly accommodation options that cater to different preferences. Consider staying in cozy guesthouses, bed and breakfasts, or even private rooms rented through

platforms like Airbnb. These alternatives often provide comfortable stays at a fraction of the cost of high-end hotels.

7. Take Advantage of Discount Cards: Look out for discount cards or passes that offer reduced prices on attractions, museums, and public transportation. These cards can provide significant savings if you plan to visit multiple attractions or use public transport extensively.

8. Enjoy Nature's Splendor: One of the biggest draws of Sorento is its breathtaking natural landscapes. Hike along the renowned Path of the Gods, explore the dramatic cliffs of Capri, or relax on the pristine beaches of the Amalfi Coast. These outdoor activities allow you to experience Sorento's beauty without spending a fortune.

By implementing these cost-saving tips and suggestions, you can make the most of your

Sorento adventure while staying within your budget. Embrace the charm, culture, and flavors of this enchanting region without worrying about excessive costs.

Chapter 4

Top attractions and activities in Sorrento

Here is some unique information about the top attractions and activities in Sorrento:

1. Explore the Historic Center: Sorrento's historic center is a delightful maze of narrow streets, lined with charming shops, cafes, and colorful buildings. Take a leisurely stroll through its picturesque lanes, discover hidden squares, and admire the beautiful architecture, such as the 15th-century Sedil Dominova.

2. Visit the Duomo di Sorrento: Located in Piazza della Vittoria, the Duomo di Sorrento is an impressive cathedral that dates back to the 15th century. Admire its ornate facade and step inside to marvel at the stunning frescoes and the beautiful bell tower. Don't miss the opportunity to explore the nearby

Cloister of San Francesco, a peaceful oasis adorned with beautiful ceramics.

3. Enjoy the Views from Villa Comunale: This charming public garden offers breathtaking views of the Bay of Naples and Mount Vesuvius. Take a leisurely stroll through the park, relax on a bench, and soak in the panoramic vistas. The Villa Comunale is also a great spot to enjoy a picnic or watch the sunset over the sea.

4. Discover the Marina Grande: Located at the bottom of a steep descent, the Marina Grande is Sorrento's charming fishing village. Wander along its colorful promenade, lined with seafood restaurants and traditional fishing boats. Relax on the beach, indulge in fresh seafood, or take a boat trip to explore the coastline.

5. Explore the Sorrento Coastline: Sorrento is the perfect base for exploring the stunning Amalfi Coast. Embark on a boat tour to

explore the rugged coastline, visit picturesque towns like Positano and Amalfi, and swim in crystal-clear waters. Alternatively, take a scenic drive along the Amalfi Coast, stopping at viewpoints to capture breathtaking vistas.

6. Visit the Museo Correale di Terranova: This museum houses an impressive collection of art and artifacts that provide insight into Sorrento's history and culture. Admire the fine porcelain, exquisite furniture, and ancient Roman artifacts. The museum is located in a beautiful villa with stunning gardens.

7. Learn Limoncello Making: Sorrento is renowned for its production of limoncello, a delicious lemon liqueur. Take a tour of a local lemon grove, learn about the cultivation of Sorrento lemons, and discover the traditional process of making limoncello. You may even get a chance to taste this zesty liqueur.

8. Hike the Path of the Gods: For outdoor enthusiasts, the Path of the Gods (Sentiero degli Dei) offers a breathtaking hiking experience. This trail winds along the cliffs of the Amalfi Coast, offering stunning views of the sea and the surrounding landscape. Be prepared for a moderate-level hike and allow plenty of time to savor the beauty of the route.

Sorrento's attractions and activities provide a captivating blend of history, natural beauty, and cultural experiences. Whether you're wandering through the charming streets, exploring ancient sites, or immersing yourself in the coastal scenery, Sorrento is sure to leave you with lasting memories.

Best time to visit Sorrento

Sorrento's Mediterranean climate blesses the region with mild, pleasant weather throughout the year. However, to truly make the most of your visit, there are a few key factors to consider. The best time to visit Sorrento depends on your personal preferences, desired activities, and tolerance for crowds.

Spring, specifically the months of April to June, emerges as an ideal period to explore Sorrento. During this time, the temperatures gradually rise, ranging from comfortably cool to pleasantly warm. The beauty of spring is witnessed in the blossoming flora, as vibrant flowers adorn the town and fill the air with a fragrant charm. You'll find fewer crowds compared to the peak summer season, allowing you to explore the attractions with more tranquility.

If you seek the epitome of summer bliss and are willing to embrace the vibrant energy of fellow travelers, July and August beckon as the prime months to experience Sorrento at its most lively. The sun shines brightly, temperatures soar, and the azure waters of the Mediterranean become inviting. Bask in the warmth of the Mediterranean sun, lounge on the stunning beaches, and savor the joyous atmosphere that permeates the town during this time. However, do bear in mind that tourist influx is at its peak, resulting in more crowded streets and bustling attractions.

For those who prefer a more serene experience and mild weather, the shoulder seasons of early autumn (September and October) and late spring (late May) present a captivating alternative. The temperatures are still comfortably warm, the summer crowds dissipate, and the prices of accommodations and flights are more favorable. Explore the charming streets, indulge in delicious cuisine, and enjoy the natural beauty of Sorrento at a more relaxed pace.

While the winter months from November to February offer a respite from the crowds, it's important to note that the town experiences a noticeable decrease in tourism during this period. The temperatures cool down, and some attractions may have limited opening hours. However, if you're a fan of tranquility, wish to delve into the local culture, and don't mind cooler temperatures, visiting Sorrento during winter can provide a unique and peaceful experience.

In conclusion, the best time to visit Sorrento ultimately depends on your personal preferences. Whether you opt for the vibrant energy of summer, the mild tranquility of the shoulder seasons, or the peaceful charm of winter, Sorrento's allure will captivate you year-round.

Outdoor activities

Here is some unique information about outdoor activities in Sorrento:

1. Hiking the Path of the Gods: For avid hikers and nature enthusiasts, the renowned Path of the Gods (Sentiero degli Dei) offers a breathtaking adventure. This scenic trail winds along the cliffs of the Amalfi Coast, offering awe-inspiring views of the sparkling Mediterranean Sea and the picturesque towns dotting the coastline. Lace up your hiking boots, breathe in the fresh coastal air, and immerse yourself in the natural beauty of this legendary path.

2. Boat Tours along the Amalfi Coast: Explore the stunning coastline of the Amalfi Coast by embarking on a boat tour from Sorrento. Sail along the azure waters, marvel at the towering cliffs, and discover hidden coves and pristine beaches. Bask in the sun, take refreshing dips in the crystal-clear sea, and create unforgettable

memories against the backdrop of this enchanting coastline.

3. Kayaking in the Bay of Naples: Experience the Bay of Naples from a unique perspective by kayaking along its serene waters. Rent a kayak and paddle your way around the coastline, admiring the dramatic cliffs, exploring hidden caves, and soaking in the tranquility of the sea. As you glide through the crystal-clear waters, you may even spot marine life such as dolphins and sea turtles.

4. Scenic Bike Rides: Rent a bicycle and embark on a scenic ride through the picturesque landscapes surrounding Sorrento. Pedal along coastal roads, pass by lemon groves and olive orchards, and soak in the breathtaking views of the Mediterranean Sea. Stop by charming villages, enjoy a leisurely picnic, and savor the freedom of exploring the region on two wheels.

5. Snorkeling and Diving: Discover the underwater wonders of the Mediterranean by engaging in snorkeling or diving adventures in Sorrento. Put on your mask, snorkel, and fins to explore vibrant marine life and colorful coral reefs. Alternatively, if you're a certified diver, join a diving excursion to explore deeper waters and encounter fascinating marine ecosystems.

6. Paragliding: Soar through the sky and experience the thrill of paragliding in Sorrento. Take in panoramic views of the coastline, the azure sea, and the charming towns nestled among the hills. Adrenaline junkies will revel in the exhilarating sensation of flying while being surrounded by the breathtaking natural beauty of the region.

7. Golfing with a View: Tee off amidst stunning vistas at the Golf Club located in Sant'Agata sui Due Golfi, just a short

distance from Sorrento. This 18-hole course offers a unique golfing experience, combining the challenge of the game with panoramic views of the Amalfi Coast and the Bay of Naples. Enjoy a leisurely day of golf while immersing yourself in the scenic surroundings.

Sorrento and its surrounding areas offer a plethora of outdoor activities that cater to various interests and levels of adventure. Whether you're hiking along dramatic cliffs, exploring the sea by kayak or boat, or indulging in thrilling aerial experiences, the natural beauty of Sorrento provides the perfect backdrop for unforgettable outdoor adventures.

Prices of top attractions and activities in Sorrento

Here is the firsthand knowledge of the costs associated with experiencing the best that Sorrento has to offer.

1. Entrance Fees for Historical Sites: Sorrento is home to several historical sites and attractions that showcase its rich heritage. The entrance fees vary depending on the specific site. For example, the Duomo di Sorrento, the town's impressive cathedral, typically has a modest entrance fee of around €3-€5. Similarly, the Museo Correale di Terranova, which houses a collection of art and artifacts, generally charges around €8-€10 for admission.

2. Boat Tours along the Amalfi Coast: Exploring the stunning Amalfi Coast by boat is a popular activity for visitors to Sorrento. The prices for boat tours can vary depending on the duration and type of tour you choose. On average, a half-day boat tour along the coastline, stopping at picturesque towns such as Positano and Amalfi, can range from €60-€100 per person. Full-day tours or private charters may have higher costs.

3. Hiking Excursions: Sorrento offers fantastic hiking opportunities, including the renowned Path of the Gods. Participating in guided hiking excursions can enhance your experience and provide insights into the local flora, fauna, and history. The prices for guided hikes can vary depending on the duration and level of difficulty. On average, a half-day guided hike along the Path of the Gods may cost around €40-€60 per person.

4. Cooking Classes and Food Experiences: To immerse yourself in the culinary delights of Sorrento, consider joining a cooking class or a food experience. Prices for these activities can vary depending on the duration, location, and the specific program. On average, a half-day cooking class, where you learn to prepare traditional dishes such as pasta and limoncello, can range from €80-€120 per person.

5. Wine Tasting and Vineyard Tours: Sorrento's surrounding countryside is

dotted with vineyards and wineries, offering opportunities to indulge in wine tasting and vineyard tours. Prices for these experiences can vary depending on the winery and the level of tasting offered. On average, a wine tasting experience with a guided tour of a vineyard may range from €20-€40 per person.

It's important to note that these prices are approximate and can vary depending on the season, availability, and any additional services or amenities included. Also, keep in mind that some attractions or activities may offer discounted rates for children or have package deals available.

 You can also explore different options, compare prices, and consider any special promotions or discounts that may be available during your visit. Additionally, don't hesitate to engage with locals and seek recommendations for hidden gems or lesser-known activities that may offer unique experiences at more affordable prices.

Chapter 5

Food and drink in Sorrento/ best restaurants

Sorrento is a gastronomic paradise, offering a wide array of delectable food and drink options that cater to all tastes. From fresh seafood to mouthwatering pasta dishes and locally produced wines, the culinary scene in Sorrento is a true delight for food enthusiasts. Here is some unique information about the food and drink scene in Sorrento, including a few of the best restaurants to visit:

1. Local Delicacies: Sorrento is known for its unique local delicacies that showcase the flavors of the region. Don't miss the opportunity to try "gnocchi alla sorrentina," a delicious dish made with potato dumplings, tomato sauce, and melted mozzarella cheese. Another must-try is "limoncello," a refreshing liqueur made from Sorrento's famous lemons.

2. Seafood Specialties: Given its coastal location, it's no surprise that Sorrento excels in seafood cuisine. Indulge in dishes like "spaghetti alle vongole" (spaghetti with clams), "frittura di paranza" (mixed fried seafood), or "pesce all'acqua pazza" (fish cooked in a flavorful broth). Visit local seafood restaurants for the freshest catch of the day.

3. Pizza Paradise: Naples, the birthplace of pizza, is just a short drive from Sorrento. Take advantage of this proximity and savor authentic Neapolitan pizza, with its thin, chewy crust and high-quality toppings. Many pizzerias in Sorrento follow traditional recipes, ensuring a truly delightful pizza experience.

4. Rustic Trattorias: For an authentic taste of local cuisine, head to one of Sorrento's charming trattorias. These rustic restaurants offer a cozy ambiance and serve

traditional dishes made with locally sourced ingredients. Don't miss out on the opportunity to try specialties like "ravioli capresi" (ravioli stuffed with caciotta cheese) or "scialatielli" (thick homemade pasta) with seafood.

5. Michelin-Starred Excellence: Sorrento is also home to a few Michelin-starred restaurants that elevate dining to a whole new level. These establishments offer exquisite menus crafted by talented chefs who showcase their culinary artistry using local ingredients. Treat yourself to a memorable gastronomic experience in a refined setting.

6. Wine Tasting: Sorrento is nestled in the Campania region, known for its exceptional wines. Explore the local vineyards and wineries to savor renowned wines such as Lacryma Christi, Fiano di Avellino, and Greco di Tufo. Many restaurants and enoteche (wine bars) offer wine tastings,

allowing you to appreciate the rich flavors and aromas of Campanian wines.

7. Gelato Galore: No visit to Sorrento is complete without indulging in some authentic Italian gelato. Wander through the streets and find gelaterias that serve a variety of flavors made with high-quality ingredients. From classic options like chocolate and pistachio to unique combinations like lemon and basil, there's a gelato flavor to satisfy every palate.

When it comes to food and drink in Sorrento, you'll find a range of options to suit every preference and budget. Whether you choose to dine in local trattorias, explore Michelin-starred establishments, or simply enjoy gelato by the sea, Sorrento promises a culinary adventure you won't forget. Buon appetito!

Best Restaurant

Here are some unique recommendations for the best restaurants in Sorrento and their approximate locations:

1. Ristorante Il Buco - Located in the heart of Sorrento's historic center, this charming restaurant offers a delightful dining experience. Il Buco is known for its creative seafood dishes and warm, welcoming atmosphere. Address: Via San Cesareo, 60, 80067 Sorrento NA, Italy.

2. O' Parrucchiano La Favorita - Situated in a beautiful garden setting, this historic restaurant is famous for its homemade pasta and traditional Sorrentine cuisine. Don't miss their signature dish, "Cannelloni alla Favorita." Address: Corso Italia, 71, 80067 Sorrento NA, Italy.

3. Ristorante Tasso - Located in the heart of Sorrento's Piazza Tasso, this elegant restaurant offers a refined dining experience. With a focus on fresh, seasonal

ingredients, Ristorante Tasso serves creative Mediterranean dishes with a modern twist. Address: Piazza Tasso, 11, 80067 Sorrento NA, Italy.

4. L'Antica Trattoria - Nestled in the picturesque Marina Grande, this family-run trattoria specializes in authentic Sorrentine cuisine. The restaurant's rustic charm, friendly service, and delicious seafood dishes make it a favorite among locals and visitors alike. Address: Via Marina Grande, 62, 80067 Sorrento NA, Italy.

5. Zi'Ntonio Mare - Situated on the waterfront promenade, Zi'Ntonio Mare offers stunning views of the Bay of Naples while serving delectable seafood and Neapolitan specialties. Enjoy a memorable dining experience with fresh catch-of-the-day options and warm hospitality. Address: Via Marina Grande, 228, 80067 Sorrento NA, Italy.

6. Il Convivio - Tucked away in a quiet alley, Il Convivio is a hidden gem known for its intimate atmosphere and creative Italian cuisine. The restaurant sources local ingredients to create dishes that reflect the flavors of the region. Address: Via Padre Reginaldo Giuliani, 33, 80067 Sorrento NA, Italy.

7. Don Alfonso 1890 - Located in nearby Sant'Agata sui Due Golfi, this world-renowned restaurant is worth the short journey from Sorrento. With three Michelin stars, Don Alfonso 1890 offers an exceptional culinary experience, blending traditional Campanian flavors with innovative techniques. Address: Corso Sant'Agata, 11/13, 80064 Sant'Agata sui Due Golfi NA, Italy.

These exceptional restaurants in Sorrento and its surroundings offer diverse culinary experiences that highlight the region's flavors and culinary traditions.

Chapter 6

Sustainable local communities and economies

Sorrento and its surrounding areas are committed to preserving the environment, supporting local businesses, and fostering sustainable practices that benefit both residents and visitors.

1. Embracing Local Agriculture: The region takes pride in its agricultural heritage, with a focus on sustainable farming practices. Local farmers cultivate traditional crops such as lemons, olives, and grapes, using organic and environmentally friendly methods. By supporting local agriculture, you not only enjoy fresh, high-quality produce but also contribute to the preservation of traditional farming practices and the local economy.

2. Promoting Local Crafts and Artisans: Sorrento is renowned for its skilled artisans

who produce beautiful crafts, including intricate woodwork, ceramics, and embroidery. These traditional crafts are not only unique and aesthetically pleasing but also sustain local businesses and preserve cultural heritage. By purchasing locally made crafts, you directly support the artisans and contribute to the continuation of these traditional crafts.

3. Sustainable Fishing Practices: As a coastal town, Sorrento has a rich fishing tradition. Local fishermen have embraced sustainable fishing practices to protect marine ecosystems and ensure the long-term viability of their industry. When dining in seafood restaurants, look for establishments that prioritize sourcing their seafood responsibly and supporting local fishermen who adhere to sustainable practices.

4. Eco-friendly Accommodations: Sorrento offers a range of eco-friendly accommodations that prioritize

sustainability. These establishments often employ energy-efficient measures, waste reduction strategies, and support local initiatives. By choosing to stay in these eco-friendly accommodations, you can contribute to reducing your environmental impact while supporting businesses that prioritize sustainability.

5. Sustainable Tourism Initiatives: The local community actively promotes sustainable tourism initiatives to preserve the natural beauty and cultural heritage of Sorrento. These initiatives include responsible tour operators, educational programs on environmental conservation, and efforts to minimize the ecological footprint of tourism activities. By engaging in sustainable tourism practices, such as respecting natural areas, conserving water and energy, and supporting local businesses, visitors can contribute to the long-term well-being of Sorrento's communities and economies.

6. Community Engagement: The local community in Sorrento is deeply involved in preserving and promoting sustainable practices. Community initiatives include beach clean-ups, tree planting campaigns, and educational programs on sustainability. Visitors are often encouraged to participate in these activities, fostering a sense of connection and shared responsibility towards the environment and the local community.

Sorrento's sustainable local communities and economies rely on the collective efforts of residents, businesses, and visitors alike.

Chapter 7

Additional resources for planning your trip to Sorrento :Sorrento map website, apps and more.

Here are a few websites, map apps, and additional resources that are popular among locals:

1. Sorrento.com: This website is a go-to resource for Sorrento locals and visitors alike. It provides comprehensive information about accommodations, restaurants, attractions, and local events. The website also offers a useful forum where you can connect with other travelers and get insider tips.

2. Moovit: Moovit is a widely used map app in Sorrento that provides real-time public transportation information. It covers bus and train routes, schedules, and even offers live updates on any delays or disruptions.

It's a great tool to help you navigate Sorrento and its surrounding areas using public transportation.

3. Italia Slow Tour - Sorrento: Italia Slow Tour is a platform dedicated to promoting sustainable and slow travel in Italy. Their Sorrento section offers a wealth of information about lesser-known attractions, scenic drives, hiking trails, and local food experiences. It's an excellent resource to discover hidden gems and off-the-beaten-path destinations.

4. Instagram: While not a specific website or app, Instagram is a treasure trove of inspiration for planning your Sorrento trip. Many locals and travel enthusiasts share their experiences, recommendations, and stunning photos of Sorrento on Instagram. You can search for hashtags like #Sorrento, #SorrentoCoast, or #VisitSorrento to discover unique places and get inspired.

5. Local Travel Blogs: Sorrento has several passionate travel bloggers who share their insights and tips for exploring the area. These blogs offer a more personal and local perspective, highlighting lesser-known attractions and authentic experiences. Some popular Sorrento travel blogs include "Sorrento Dreams" (sorrentodreams.com) and "Sorrento Insider" (sorrentoinsider.com/blog).

6. Local Tourism Offices: When in Sorrento, be sure to visit the local tourism office. They can provide you with brochures, maps, and personalized recommendations based on your interests. The staff at these offices are knowledgeable about the area and can offer valuable insights and suggestions for your itinerary.

7. Ask the Locals: One of the best resources available to you is the friendly people of Sorrento. Don't hesitate to strike up conversations with locals, whether it's at a

café, restaurant, or while exploring the town. They can offer insider tips, recommend hidden gems, and provide a genuine local perspective that you won't find in any guidebook.

By utilizing these resources, you'll be able to plan a truly unique and immersive experience in Sorrento.

Conclusion

In conclusion, Sorrento stands as a captivating destination that captivates visitors with its stunning coastal landscapes, rich cultural heritage, and warm Mediterranean charm. From its breathtaking views of the Amalfi Coast to its delicious cuisine and warm hospitality, Sorrento offers a truly unforgettable travel experience.

As you explore Sorrento, you'll be immersed in a tapestry of ancient history, vibrant local communities, and sustainable practices. From the sun-kissed beaches and crystal-clear waters to the enchanting streets lined with artisan shops and cafes, Sorrento invites you to indulge in its unique blend of natural beauty and cultural treasures.

Whether you choose to visit during the lively summer months, when the town comes alive with energy, or prefer the tranquility of the shoulder seasons, Sorrento has something to offer every traveler. From hiking along scenic trails and embarking on boat tours along the coast to savoring the local flavors and engaging in sustainable tourism initiatives, Sorrento presents a myriad of opportunities to create cherished memories.

As you venture through this coastal gem, take the time to engage with the local community, discover their traditions, and support their sustainable initiatives. By embracing the local culture and contributing to the local economy, you become an active participant in the preservation of Sorrento's natural beauty and vibrant way of life.

Whether you seek relaxation, adventure, or a taste of the dolce vita, Sorrento invites you to embark on a journey that will leave a lasting impression. So pack your bags, immerse yourself in the wonders of Sorrento, and let this captivating destination captivate your heart and soul.

Happy travels!

Made in the USA
Middletown, DE
03 August 2023